IT Governance

for

CEOs

and

Members of the Board

I0473782

Bryn Phillips B.Com, CGEIT, CISA, CISM

Copyright © 2012 Bryn Phillips
ISBN: 1475035381
ISBN 13: 978-1475035384

Contents

Foreword

By Professor Mervyn King SC

Chair of the King Committee on Corporate Governance

Over the last twenty years, with an increasing number of natural disasters, recessions, corporate scandals and substantial pressures on organisations to improve social and environmental responsibility, there has been particular emphasis on the need for better Corporate Governance. IT Governance and Security is a key element.

King III has emphasised how pervasive Information Technology has become in the business model and that, in itself, mandates the governance of IT as a corporate imperative.

Providing the necessary reasonable care and due diligence in regard to IT's Governance and Security, Bryn Phillips has identified, demystified and explained some of the major elements. He has placed them within the context of an overall framework and an organisation structure, together with appropriate committees (with agreed charters). He has established the necessity of IT Governance and Security being a Board agenda item and he has given some guidance and recommendations on what directors need to do for themselves and what they should delegate and expect others to do on their behalf. One must remember, however, that directors can delegate but they cannot abdicate their responsibilities.

Specific focus has been given to the alignment between the strategic plan and IT. Responsibility for the operation of IT systems has, correctly, been placed on individual line management.

Mr Phillips has not disappointed in making value delivery a key concept for directors. He stresses the need for governance of both capital and operational expenditure with careful measurement of benefits, both tangible and intangible, in the (agile) building of software assets (software development) and in the provision of on-going operational services (computer operations).

He has addressed the identification of information assets and the confidentiality, integrity, availability and privacy issues; the need for risk management using specialist knowledge; the importance of people (and the need to consider their skills and behaviour), processes, and technologies in the resource structure; and he has emphasised the monitoring and reporting of performance at both the strategic and the operational level.

Compliance is approached in two ways. First of all, recognising what to comply with (general business laws, specific industry focus, standards and internal organisational requirements); and secondly, ensuring that compliance is actually taking place.

Finally, he has stressed the need for the Board to have some method of independent assurance through internal audit, external audit and third parties. [Sarbanes-Oxley legislation in the USA has been analysed for its impact on Information Technology, although the legislation itself does not address IT as a specific issue.]

It is impossible, in a few short pages, to address all the IT Governance issues that affect CEOs and Board members but Mr Phillips has given an interesting introduction to the topic and, for most directors, much room for thought.

Mervyn King SC
Johannesburg
February 2012

Acknowledgements

This book would not have been possible without the input from a vast body of knowledge, drawn from colleagues and peers around the world. There has been many a debate and discussion in various forums, and all of this has assisted in bringing this book to fruition. In addition the following frameworks, guides and documents, amongst others, were used as reference material and input for this book.

ISACA & ITGI CobiT V4.1 and V5

ITIL 2011

ISO Standards, Particularly 38500:2008

King Code of Governance Principles (King III)

Sarbanes-Oxley Act: 2002

My thanks to my employers and The Pacific Institute and their programs for giving me the tools and motivation to finish what I had started.

Professor Mervyn King made his valuable time available to not only pen the foreword, but also took the time to read and comment on this book. This is truly appreciated.

Finally to my family, Jenny, Cassidy and Devony. I am sorry that this book took me away from you while I worked on it. Thank you for your patience and understanding.

Introduction

Well Done!!! You've worked hard for a number of years, you've sacrificed the hours, you've taken the risks, and now you've made it to the top of your game. Sure, there will still be ups and downs, but mostly you should be able to enjoy the view from the top.

Trouble is, along the way you've picked up some partners (stakeholders for those of you already into this sort of thing), and now, instead of doing the business of your business, you have got to spend an unreasonable proportion of your time and a significant portion of your resources appeasing and pandering to all the whims of these stakeholders.

All this Corporate Governance stuff has, for most of you, now become law. You have to do it. That is why this book can be written. If it were not for all the fuss, you would not even have given this title a second glance.

So why IT Governance? Why not Sales and Marketing Governance? – those guys can spend a fortune and revenues stay flat or even decline. Besides, if you have no sales you have no business. Why not HR Governance? Surely people are important?

The answer is fairly simple. IT is pervasive. It is immersed and intertwined in every aspect of your business. It is also not generally well understood. The source, the processing, the calculation and presentation of your financial results (which is one of the key elements of Corporate Governance) are all done through your IT systems, and are reliant on those systems. As for the rest of the business, there are likely to be few aspects that do not touch IT, and the execution of all the business processes are not only going to use IT, but rely and depend on IT for their completion. The fact is that if IT fails, then it is highly likely that the business (or that part of the business) will fail.

The King III report on Governance introduces it as follows:

"Information systems were used as enablers to business, but have now become pervasive in the sense that they are built into the strategy of the business. The pervasiveness of IT in business today mandates the governance of IT as a corporate imperative."

In fact, the King Report on Governance devotes an entire chapter (chapter 5 of 9 chapters) to IT Governance, giving an indication of the importance placed on this discipline.

There is a certain amount of mystery and mystique around Information Technology, and it is a field that requires specialized knowledge. It is this mystery and perhaps the discontent that Executives, Board Members and other stakeholders associate with not fully understanding the technology, its processes and the impacts that it has that led to the drive towards increased requirements for IT Governance.

Your stakeholders want to know that you are taking reasonable care of this critical aspect of the business, in order to ensure that the business continues to operate.

As for the others, we all know that the touchy feely HR crowd really have to consciously make an effort to have a negative impact on the business, and the silver-tongued marketing gurus, by their very nature, can sell any project to management or the board. So when concerns are raised about marketing, they just talk their way out of it. Unfortunately, most of the IT geeks that became management never really got the hang of this marketing stuff, so they weren't able to talk themselves out of the predicament that is IT.

And let's face it, when things go well nobody notices, but one minor glitch, and all hell breaks loose. Besides, the technology industry's track record is not that great. There was the whole Y2K thing that cost a fortune, and nobody was really able to, or dared, to show that if they had done nothing, everything would have worked anyway. There is also the whole planned obsolescence thing, which was not necessarily planned, but has just turned out that way.

According to Moore's Law, processing capacity doubles at least every 18 months, so there is this whole vicious cycle of upgrades, obsolescence and technology refresh. Besides, technology is not cheap. Technology spend is often a significant chunk of many corporations' capital and operational expenditure. There have also been numerous incidents of IT failures that have resulted in embarrassment, cost and sometimes even failure of the business.

Let's look at the whole Sony credit card incident. I would like to think that Sony would not only have taken reasonable steps to protect its data, but also would have taken extraordinary measures to do so. Despite those steps and measures, determined, intelligent and persistent individuals still managed to breach their defenses, with the resultant embarrassment, costs and declining revenues.

It is not likely to result in the closure of Sony, but it certainly would have caused their CEO and Members of the Board many sleepless nights and much distress.

To draw from the experience of Sony, be aware that implementing IT Governance processes, and implementing them well, may not protect you from all threats and risks, but it will reduce the chances of this sort of thing happening, and will provide you with the ability to respond appropriately.

It will also allow you to cast one worry from your mind, knowing that, as far as your IT processes are concerned, you personally have taken due care and diligence to provide, (in the words of the IT Governance Institute), "...

the leadership and organizational structures and processes that ensure that the organization's IT sustains and extends the organization's strategies and objectives."

The objective of this book is to provide you with the knowledge to do what you have to do to ensure that IT Governance within your organization is at a level that will be acceptable to your stakeholders. You are busy (or at least you should be), so this book is written, not as a detailed guide, nor as an educational thesis, but to provide you with an overview of what you need to do, in order that you can delegate to your management, but at the same time, understand what it is that you are delegating.

This book is also intended for use around the globe, so while references may be made to specific legislation, codes or reports, the principles discussed will be generic, and should be applicable across jurisdictions.

Knowing that the bulk of board members and CEOs will be on the wrong side of the age requiring reading glasses, it is also written in a large font, to facilitate the ease of reading. Given that most of you will not be from an IT background, and given the technological jargon that makes up the language of IT, the jargon and TLAs (Three Letter Acronyms) have been avoided where possible.

Disclaimer

It is an unfortunate reality of the modern world that there is an increased propensity to litigate, and in order to provide protection against civil or other liability a disclaimer is necessary.

Therefore, let it be known that the author, publishers, agents, employers, employees, or any other person or organization involved in the delivery of this content will not be liable for any direct, indirect, special or consequential loss or damages of any nature related to the use of this content, either through acts of omission or commission or any other cause. There is no warranty or contract implied, given or agreed to. Use of this content is at the readers own risk and reward.

IT Governance Defined

IT Governance is a subset of Corporate Governance. Every definition of Corporate Governance that you have come across can be applied or extended to IT Governance. I am not going into those here.

There are at least two definitions for every IT Governance practitioner. I have got about five, but will stick to the simplest. I referred to it earlier. It is the definition given in the IT Governance Institute's document "Board Briefing on IT Governance" and is as follows.

"IT governance is the responsibility of the board of directors and executive management. It is an integral part of enterprise governance and consists of the leadership and organizational structures and processes that ensure that the organization's IT sustains and extends the organization's strategies and objectives."

In short, IT Governance ensures that IT is efficient and effective, and meets the needs of the organisation. That is my two definitions done. One and a bit pages only!!

Responsibility for IT Governance

You know that you are responsible otherwise you wouldn't be reading this book. What you may not know is that you can delegate this responsibility.

You are not expected to run the IT department. That is the job of your CIO (Sorry, a TLA – Chief Information Officer). You are also not expected to inspect every single detail of that function. That can become the function of various IT committees (of the board or otherwise). Those committees would of course have to report to the Board, in order that you can satisfy yourselves that due care and diligence has been applied in running the department.

So let's cover a few of these committees. You should already be familiar with committees. Many of these have been prescribed as part of various Corporate Governance codes and reports. There are a plethora of them. Risk

Committee, Audit Committee, Remuneration Committee, Strategy Committee, Executive Committee, etc.

The IT Governance Frameworks (which will be covered later on in the book) call for a number of IT committees to manage and oversee the function. These may be Board or Management Committees, depending on your jurisdiction, and all of them have a specific purpose.

Each Committee will require a charter. Your CIO should prepare these charters, but will in all probability battle with this concept, so get help from those that developed the charters for all your other committees. A detailed write up of each of these IT Committees was being considered for this book, but in the interests of brevity, they will just be listed, and guidance concerning your handling of them will follow.

- IT Steering Committee
- IT Strategy Committee
- IT Governance Committee

- IT Standards Committee
- IT Technology Council
- IT Architecture Review Board

This is just the start of the IT Committees that exist. As you can see, they are many and varied, and you have to ask yourself when does your CIO get a chance to do any actual work? The level of these committees also varies, and some are defined as Board, others Executive, and still others as Management Committees.

From a Board perspective, you only want to deal with a single committee that covers all the aspects of IT that your jurisdiction requires. Call it the IT Committee or Board IT Committee, and ensure that your CIO prepares its charter to encompass all of those required aspects. The CIO should then be left to structure the balance of the committees at executive and management level so that they are appropriate for the needs of your organisation.

Depending on the size of your organization, and the complexity of coordinating the diaries of the Board members, you may wish to include the charter of your new IT Committee in one of your other committees, such as the Risk Committee or Audit Committee, or at least schedule the meetings to precede or follow on from one of the others.

All of the other IT Committees at executive and management level should then report into the Board IT Committee.

In summary, in terms of **Responsibility for IT Governance**, you have to do the following.

1. Ensure IT and IT Governance are Board Agenda items.
2. Appoint a Board IT Committee and delegate responsibilities to it.

In light of the seriousness and attention being given to IT Governance at Board level, it would certainly be prudent and proactive to appoint your CIO to the Board, if you have not already done so. There are enough reasons to warrant this, especially in terms of responsibility and ensuring that all critical aspects of IT are brought to the attention of the Board. If your current CIO is not suitable to be a member of the Board (even if they do not become a member of the Board), then you should consider whether they are in fact suitable for the role of CIO and capable of assuming the huge responsibility for IT.

The IT Governance Framework

Many of the governance codes and reports require that you have a framework that deals with your IT Governance processes. This is a fairly reasonable thing to ask for. Rather have a recognized set of structures than rely on something that has been developed internally on an ad hoc basis. At this time, however, there is no set standard as to what that framework is, and how it should be implemented. It must also be considered that these frameworks are guides, not standards, and measurement of compliance to these guides is a judgmental assessment, rather than an absolute yes / no scenario.

In addition, the frameworks recognize that there is no "one size fits all" solution, and allow for selection of appropriate components of the framework. They also recognize that different organizations will implement them differently and to varying degrees. These differences are measured in terms of maturity models that work on a standard set of criteria. This will allow for measurement of improvements internally, as well as comparison with other external organizations.

Again, it is not the intention to provide too much detail of these frameworks, but to provide guidance as to what you should do about them.

CobiT

This is a framework developed by the IT Governance Institute and ISACA. It is a process based framework, and provides a detailed description of the activities that should be taking place within your IT structures, and also provides the tools to measure the maturity of the implementation. It does not refer to or rely on any technology and should fit for all organizations. It is developed and maintained by internationally diverse teams of people, and adapts to changing circumstances. It has been accepted and implemented across the globe. This book draws extensively on this framework and related materials.

ITIL

This is a framework enthusiastically adopted by many IT departments. Its primary focus is Service Delivery along with the related processes. It is not necessarily a Governance Framework, but adopting ITIL is good practice.

ISO 38500

This is an ISO standard, based primarily on input from the Australian IT Governance standard. This deals with IT Governance at an extremely high level, and deals with a number of principles, most of which are treated as headings in this book, and covers the activities involved with the processes of Evaluate, Direct and Monitor.

There are a number of other standards and documents out there, but the above are probably the most commonly used.

In summary, your responsibilities concerning the **IT Governance Framework** are as follows.

1.) You need to ask your CIO what framework governs the IT operations
2.) You need to establish the credibility of that framework and the extent to which it is implemented and accepted elsewhere.
3.) You need your CIO to measure and report on the extent to which they have adopted the framework, or the maturity level at which they operate.

The Elements of IT Governance

IT Governance involves a number of elements, (the number will vary depending on which framework you are looking at). The elements that follow are drawn from a number of frameworks and guides. There is some overlap between them, and there are differing terminologies for what is essentially the same process.

This book will attempt to provide a guide to them, as succinctly as possible, which will give you an idea of what they are about, what you have to do about them (To Do)and what you should be looking for to ensure those elements are in place(To Demand).

Thankfully, most of the time, you will be able to, and in fact should, delegate the hard work contained within the elements to your CIO, and get him or her to report to the board.

Responsibility for IT Governance

You may wonder why this has been included a second time. The reason for discussion above is that it is probably the most important aspect of IT Governance, and the IT Governance processes will not proceed without your acceptance of responsibility, and without you driving those processes. The reason it is included in this section is for the sake of completeness because many of the frameworks treat this as one of the elements of their governance processes.

To Do

1.) Formally assume responsibility for IT Governance
2.) Ensure IT and IT Governance are standing items on the Board Agenda
3.) Appoint a Board IT Committee and delegate responsibilities to it.

To Demand

1.) A report from the Board IT Committee to the Board, that provides the required information that allows you to discharge your duties and responsibilities for IT Governance.

Alignment of IT with the Business

This element is also often referred to as "Strategic Alignment with the Business" however the scope of IT and Business alignment extends beyond strategy.

This second element has become a little bit contentious. All of the frameworks talk about this, however CobiT version 5 has removed this as a process but has ascribed it an attribute status, and as a goal. Simply put, nobody has the job of Aligning IT with the Business, but all of the processes that IT undertake, must be aligned to the business, its needs and objectives. Many of the processes should therefore be described as aligned with the business. Examples include:

- The IT Strategic plan is aligned with the business strategic plan.
- The IT projects are geared towards meeting business objectives.

- The IT processes add value to the Business.

This section will therefore, at the risk of repetition in other elements, cover those areas where alignment with the business is required.

Strategy

This is often cited as the most important requirement, as the IT strategy drives the rest of the IT processes. The requirement is that the IT Strategy is aligned with the business strategy.

The first thing you therefore have to do, is ensure that there is a business strategy to align to. Without a business strategy there is no good basis to complete the IT strategy (or any other operational departmental strategy for that matter) and IT may end up diverting its resources to areas that do not entirely meet the needs of the business.

The next thing you have to do is make sure that your CIO and your IT Strategy

Committee (in whatever form – refer to the section on committees above) have sight of your business strategy, so they can ensure that IT strategy meets the needs and objectives of the business.

When it comes to setting goals for your strategic documents, the CobiT framework is most helpful. It documents generic business goals based on the balanced scorecard under the four perspectives of:

- Financial Perspective
- Customer Perspective
- Internal Perspective
- Learning & Growth Perspective

It then maps IT Goals to those business goals, and thereafter maps to processes, activities and control objectives that assist in meeting those IT Goals, and subsequently meeting business goals.

It gets quite complicated and detailed, and is the one area where you absolutely delegate to your CIO. Using CobiT as a guide will assist in ensuring that the strategy documents are aligned.

What you have to do is ask for sight of the IT strategy document and satisfy yourself that you understand it and that it will meet the needs of your business.

What should always be considered is that these strategy documents are planning documents to give the business direction. Along with budgets, these documents are not law, and are not cast in stone. Your business should be flexible enough, and have the processes in place to ensure that the strategy and plans are reviewed and updated on a regular basis, and if circumstances dictate, your business should be agile enough to be able to change strategies and plans in response to changing circumstances. This is crucial, especially with technology, where advances are launched on a regular basis. The mobile revolution is an example of this, where, in a very short period of time, the innovation of the iPad changed the way we work.

Risk

This is an area which is also covered later, but suffice to say, the IT risks must be analyzed in context of the business, rather than in isolation as an IT Risk.

Value

IT projects and initiatives must be geared towards meeting the needs of the business, and must provide value to the business. Using business IT resources to calculate the value of Pi to the nth decimal place, and other cool geeky projects may have merit, but are unlikely to add value to the business. Value also has its own section.

Ownership

Unless you are in the business of IT, IT is not what the business is about. The various IT systems will be in place to perform some business function, whether it be accounting (Owned by the CFO), inventory (Owned by your Inventory Controller), payroll (Owned by the Human Resources Manager), or whatever. That business function will be the responsibility of some individual manager, and that manager must be the owner of the system. The business operation will feel the impact if things go wrong with that system. Granted, there are systems that are purely for IT purposes, and in those cases, the owner will be your CIO.

Business ownership of systems should be clearly defined, and that is your responsibility to ensure that this happens.

To Do

1.) Enable mechanisms that will incorporate IT into the business, and will create the climate that will allow IT to align with the business.

To Demand

1.) Require that business management take ownership of the systems that support their processes.
2.) Ensure that the benefit to or impact on the business and its objectives is considered for all IT related matters that cross your desk, irrespective of whether they are strategic, tactical, operational or not.

Value Delivery

This is also referred to in a variety of ways, including

"Ensure Value Optimization" (CobiT 5)

"Acquisition" (ISO 38500)

Fundamentally this element concerns itself with ensuring that IT spend provides value to the business and is geared towards meeting the objectives of the business.

There are two areas of IT Value delivery. These essentially relate to expenditure of a capital and operational nature respectively.

CobiT summarizes this as

"Managing IT enabled investment programmes and other IT assets and services to ensure they deliver the greatest possible value in supporting the enterprises strategy and objectives"

Why is there the emphasis on ensuring IT Value delivery? Most likely the reason is that historically IT projects have been notorious for scope creep, budget overruns, abandonment, non delivery of the expected benefits as well as the rapid obsolescence of the investment due to rapid improvements in technology . No sooner has a project been completed (if you are lucky) than it is rendered obsolete due to marvelous innovations by all and sundry.

It is for all the above reasons that you have to keep your eye on the investments, and ensure that the promised benefits are realized, and that they remain a value proposition.

Practically of course, the evaluation and monitoring of your IT investments should be no different to any other investment, whether it be a capital project such as a factory or office block, or a marketing campaign. The discussion that follows could apply equally to all of those, and if you are not using the elements we discuss for all your capital investments, then you should consider doing so.

Capital IT Investments

Objectives

The first thing to be clear about when you sign off on the motivation for IT (or any) Capital Expenditure is the business objectives that the project is geared towards. Part of the documentation should include the specific objectives from both the IT and the business strategy document that are being addressed, to ensure that expenditure stays on track. Having said that, take cognizance of the changing landscape and external factors that may require a strategy change.

Benefits

The next thing to be clear about are the promised benefits that the investment will deliver. IT has historically provided obscure benefits such as "improved efficiency" or "improved performance" as motivation for the expenditure. You need to ensure that you clearly understand what the benefits are. They need to be clearly and precisely defined. They need to be measurable. It must also be noted it is often not possible to place a direct dollar value on the benefits derived from IT expenditure. Much of IT expenditure is related to risk reduction, such as Anti-Virus software or Disaster Recovery facilities, and therefore the benefit needs to be measured in terms of the resulting reduction in residual risk. Alternatively, the benefit can be measured in terms of the potential cost saving that would be achieved if the risk event occurs, and the controls are effective. Of course, you will only really find out if your investment provided value if the risk event actually occurs.

Benefits Measurement

Apart from being clearly defined, it must be possible to measure the benefits. The motivation should include the processes that will be used to measure those promised benefits, as well as the criteria which determine success or failure, or go-no-go scenarios. If during the implementation of the expenditure it is established that the benefits will be materially different to the original expectation, then the ongoing feasibility of the project should be considered. Also to be included are the post implementation benefit measurement processes and periods, to ensure that the investment continues to perform. As above, non-dollar benefits should also be measured where possible and the value of the investment monitored.

Cost

The costs of capital item are a critical part of the evaluation process. These need to be clearly defined, and your CIO's experience should provide him with the insight to ensure that all costs including hidden and ongoing operational costs are considered. Similarly to the ongoing benefits measurement, the costs incurred need to be monitored closely, and as soon as deviations are found (and they will be found) the feasibility should be reviewed. If the costs change to such an extent that the expected benefits no longer justify that expenditure, then the project should be considered for termination. This consideration should include benefits achieved to date, actual costs lost, as well as the costs that remain to be spent. Ongoing operational costs must also be monitored to ensure that the project continues to be viable.

Application Development

Sometimes hidden in your IT operational costs is a function that in fact creates assets for you. At least, that is the theory.

In all probability, you will have a team of software or application developers, business analysts, quality assurers and many more. Slaving away at their terminals all day, they are creating applications for you. Maybe they are changing them, maybe they are adding to them and maybe they are supporting them. Irrespective of what they are specifically doing, their costs are an investment in a Software Asset which you now own and have to manage.

Therefore, if this is an investment, you should be applying the same rules to what they do as you do to your normal capital expenditure.

While it may not be necessary for you to be aware of every little bit of application they create, you do want to know that what they are doing, supports the organization's strategy, and is geared towards achieving organizational objectives. So the same things apply as above.

Objectives

Each application development project, even the Ad Hoc ones, should be scrutinized to ensure that it supports the achievement of specific organizational goals and strategies.

Costs, Benefits and Measurement

As per the above, the costs, benefits and the mechanisms to measure these must be defined for each application development project. The difference here is that you may choose to ensure that the apportioned costs of the development team are included as part of the capital cost.

Timing

This is one area where the length of the implementation of the project must be considered. Unlike capital projects to create assets such as buildings, factories, production facilities, etc., where the benefits can be realized over many years, application development can be made obsolete before a project is complete, due to the rapid changes to technology. An example of this is where the introduction of the iPad and similar devices has changed the way we deal with our customers. Rather than have a project take a few years to complete, it should be broken down into smaller projects with shorter delivery times, allowing for benefits to be realized sooner, and also allowing the scope of the project to change to allow for changes in technology.

Your architecture, organizational structure, infrastructure, processes and capabilities should all allow for this agile method of development, thereby creating a function that is able to rapidly respond, not only to changing technologies, but also to other changing conditions such as economic, regulatory, environmental, etc.

Operational Expenditure

Your IT function will be providing your organization with some form of ongoing service. There will of course be a cost associated with the provision of this service. What IT Governance requires you to do, is to ensure that you review the following on a regular basis:

Services

Ensure that you still require all the services that your IT function offers. You may find, for example, that you purchased an application or device some time ago, but the need for that application or device has fallen away (for a number of possible reasons). You may well find that you still pay license and support fees for the product, even though it has no current benefit.

Service Delivery

Ensure that the services that you are paying for are being delivered, or are capable of being delivered. It is possible, for example, that you are paying for a 24/7/365 support contract, but no IT staff are on duty over weekends or holidays, so you wouldn't know there was a problem at those times anyway. Ensure that response times are realistic, and that your service providers (internal and external) have the resources and capabilities to meet their service obligations.

Cost / Benefits

Ensure that the benefits derived from ongoing operational expenditure are still within the approved feasibilities. In other words, ensure that you are still getting value for the costs you are incurring.

To Do

1.) Ensure that capital expenditure processes consider the organizational strategies and objectives.
2.) Ensure that the processes clearly define the benefits to be achieved, as well as the mechanisms to measure those benefits
3.) Ensure that the process allows for the full disclosure of all costs (capital and ongoing) and that there are mechanisms to monitor both cost and benefits realization.

To Demand

1.) That any internal application development is treated as a capital project, and that costs are correctly allocated to ensure correct cost benefit analyses.

2.) That operational expenditure is reviewed on a regular basis, to ensure that it is still appropriate, and that the benefits received justify the costs incurred.

Resource Management

"Resource management is the process that oversees the investment, use and allocation of IT resources, to ensure that adequate and sufficient IT related resources are available to support enterprise objectives effectively at optimal cost." (CobiT 4 & 5)

That was quite a mouthful, and it seems quite similar to the "Value Delivery" topic just covered. It is similar. The difference however relates to ensuring that the resources are appropriate to meet the service delivery requirements. These resources can be People, Processes, and Technologies (in one form or another) and this IT Governance process aims to ensure that they are appropriate.

An example of this would be the staffing of a 24-hour call centre. This call centre may have been justified on a cost benefit basis, but that justification may have only included staff for two 12-hour shifts, not three 8-hour shifts.

(assuming that 12-hour shifts are not permitted). Thus, this process would ensure that the appropriate number of staff are allocated. Your ongoing Value Delivery process should then at some point identify the cost change, and force a re-evaluation of the benefits.

This process would also cover areas of technological resources such as ensuring that the appropriate resources are available to provide the ongoing correct capacity and performance of the IT investment.

The resources required in response to changes in the organization (growth or decline) would be identified and reported on at this point. An increase in the volume of transactions may, for example, require additional disk capacity and faster processes.

To Do

1.) Ensure that processes are in place that will allow for the identification of changes in resource requirements and provide the means to address those changes.

To Demand

1.) Assurance that the IT resources are adequate for the needs of the organization, and that they are optimized.

Information Asset Management

This is a process that, unlike any of the others, is not so much technological in nature, but operational. Your information assets are those elements of data and information that reside on the technology your CIO looks after. This information belongs to the business, and is the domain of the business owners. Your information assets include the obvious, such as customer data, inventories, intellectual property, but also includes the less obvious, such as your policies and processes, and of course, your user data. Also, do not forget that much of the data in your systems is a record of the business you have done.

While much time and effort is devoted to the management of data in formal data systems, it is often forgotten that much of your business runs on informal user defined systems, that include spreadsheets (for reporting and analysis) documents, images and other user generated and managed data.

Once again, as a CEO or Member of the Board, it would not be expected of you to delve into all the data and information assets that may exist in your organization. It is however your responsibility to ensure, and to get assurance from your delegatee (if such a word exists) in the form of your IT Committee or CIO, that the Information Assets of the company are well managed.

There are a number of elements surrounding Information Asset Management, and your CIO or IT Committee should be in a position to advise you on the status of all of these.

Identification of Information Assets

Does your company actually know what information it has, and the value thereof? Before you can manage something, you need to know what it is you are managing. You (the business) should know that you have, for example, customer information, inventory information, spreadsheets, logos, trademarks, etc, all of which play a differing role in the running of your business, and has a differing value to the organization. Your information assets need to be identified and documented, along with the business owner of that information, as well as the relevance and value to the business.

Confidentiality

Now that you know (or your CIO knows) what information you have, you have to ensure that the confidentiality of that information is adequately protected. There is certain information that you will happily publish on your website for all and sundry to browse and scratch through, however there is certain information that should only be made available to a select few individuals. Your CIO should assure you that appropriate steps have been taken to ensure that your information assets do not get into the wrong hands. Imagine if the Coca Cola or Kentucky Fried Chicken recipes were generally published on the web. (Well, actually a quick

Google will find you many variations of both of those, but whether they are genuine or not is another matter)

Privacy

Many countries now have laws to protect the privacy of information. Thus, you have to ensure that you do not pass on your customer information to third parties (unless expressly authorized to do so), and that personal information (the definitions of which are many and varied) is adequately protected.

Availability

Your information is no good if you cannot access it. It is also no good to you if you can access it, but only days or weeks after you need it. Your CIO should therefore assure you that processes are in place to ensure that the information you have will be available, when you need it.

This encompasses a number of concepts, including High Availability measures,

Disaster Recovery measures and Performance Optimizing measures. All of these need to be in place in order to meet this requirement.

<u>Integrity</u>

Your information stored on your various systems will be no good to you if it is inaccurate, missing or corrupt. There should be processes in place to ensure accuracy and integrity of the information. You should also look to your Internal Audit function to provide assurance on the application and process controls, as well as to provide assurance on the reliability of your data.

<u>To Do</u>

1.) Ensure that your business operations are aware of the information assets that they are custodians of, and that they are aware of the value, importance and relevance of that information.

2.) Delegate the responsibility for Information Asset Management to your CIO, IT Committee, or both.

To Demand

1.) Assurance that the Confidentiality, Integrity and Availability (CIA) of your information is protected
2.) Assurance that the Privacy of information, particularly personal information, remains intact.
3.) Assurance that the value, importance and relevance of your information assets is identified and acknowledged by both your business management and your CIO / IT Committee

Risk Management

I am sure that at this point of your journey through these pages you are telling yourself that you have had risk management, risk committees, risk practitioners and risk generally up to your eyeballs, and certainly do not need any more missives, articles, documents or advice on risk management processes!

Quite right!

I agree with you totally.

That is why this section is going to be very brief.

The processes you follow for IT Risk Management should be THE SAME as those you follow for your General Risk Management.

The only caveat that I will add, is that you need to be aware that identifying and managing the risks relating to Information

Technology requires SPECIALIST KNOWLEDGE which does not usually reside with your general risk managers and practitioners. You need to ensure that your IT risks have been identified, assessed, and treated by people with the appropriate specialist IT knowledge.

Having said that there was one caveat, I am going to add another. You will remember very early on in this book it was identified that IT is immersed and intertwined in every aspect of your business.

It is therefore imperative that you obtain assurance that disaster recovery and business continuity processes are documented, in place and fit for purpose, not only for your IT function, but also for those operational units that depend on IT.

To Do

1.) Ensure that IT risks are managed using the same processes as your other risks.
2.) Ensure that the IT risks have been dealt with by people with the appropriate specialist knowledge.

To Demand

1.) IT risk reporting to be included in your general risk reporting.
2.) Your CIO / IT Committee / Risk Committee must regularly assure and demonstrate that disaster recovery and business continuity processes are in place and fit for purpose.

(Three pages – not too bad for a topic that has had volumes written about it)

Performance Measurement

This is an element that allows you to assess the operation and performance of your IT function. There are two aspects to this.

The first relates to an earlier discussion regarding strategy. You will have had sight of, and perhaps even approved the IT Strategic Plan. This plan would have had objectives, so now you have a mechanism against which to measure your IT Function. Your IT management structures should report to the board on a regular basis about the progress made towards achieving those goals.

The report should identify whether or not those goals are met, late, missed, exceeded or abandoned, the reasons, and the remedial action taken, if any.

The second aspect relates to the operational performance of your IT Function. Here you need your CIO to identify 5 to 10 criteria, in addition to the usual financial and general business measures, that will indicate how well the IT Function is performing. I am not even going to attempt to prescribe any of these, as they will be determined by what it is your department does. They could include variations on measures such as Downtime, Service Desk Calls, Green IT, Security Breaches, etc. CobiT provides a plethora of indicators. Some of these could be chosen.

Do not have too many, and ensure that you understand how they indicate IT performance, and also ensure that you understand the impact on the business if those indicators are not met.

To Do

   1.) Work with your CIO / IT Committee to determine indicators that will measure the performance of the IT Function

To Demand

   1.) Regular reporting on the status of the achievement of Strategic Goals.

2.) Regular reporting on the status of agreed indicators, thus measuring the performance of the IT Function.

You could of course base your CIO's and his management team's performance bonus, or part of their performance bonus on the achievement of strategic goals and the status of the agreed indicators.

Conformance / Compliance

When dealing with Compliance and IT Governance, there is no reason why IT should be singled out for different or preferential treatment. The Compliance element is included by a number of models as part of the IT Governance process. It should however be treated no differently from a Corporate Governance perspective, to any other operating department. I have no doubt that you already have some form of compliance function within your organization, whether it be part of Legal or an independent department. This compliance function should be doing the following for you.

You should know what you have to be compliant with. Due to the diversity of businesses in a variety of jurisdictions that will hopefully make use of this book, it is not possible to provide specific details about what you have to comply with, but I will cover some of this in general terms.

1. You have to comply with the general business laws of the jurisdictions in which you operate. This is where I can provide some information relating to IT Governance.

    1.1. Privacy Laws – Many countries are now regulating the protection of the private information held by organizations such as your own. This private information can include Personal Information, Medical Records, Payroll Information, Correspondence, etc. Your regulations will probably have a definition of the information to be protected. This impacts on IT Governance in that this information is usually held within your computer systems, and your CIO must ensure that it is suitably protected, and not accessible to all and sundry. This includes ensuring that remote information (such as on mobile phones, laptops, tablets ,home pc's, etc.) is also protected. This means that the volumes of customer information your sales team have on their mobile devices must not be compromised if that device is lost or stolen. It also means that the contact information synchronized between mobile phones and office productivity suites, is protected on those mobile phones in the event that they are lost or stolen.

1.2. Consumer Protection laws may require some onerous business processes, and these too are usually dealt with through the processes within your computer systems. This legislation also covers areas such as unsolicited mail, (spam). Your computer and manual processes should ensure that you do not bombard your customers with marketing information, unless they have given you explicit permission to do so. (This permission can be facilitated by that information being held within their customer record on your computer system). You should also ensure that your marketing teams do not make use of providers of external customer leads, unless you can be certain that those customers, (and your potential future customers) have given the provider explicit permission to do so.

1.3. Data or Record Retention is an area where you could be susceptible to risk if you are reliant on your computer systems to retain your records. If you have boxes and boxes of paper documents stored in a large storage facility off site, then this section will not apply to you. Most of the information required to be retained is however likely to be within your computer systems. It is possible that your jurisdiction may require you to keep information for up to 15 years or even longer. By the very nature of computer systems, they are not likely to keep everything on-line forever, as this would bring your systems to a grinding halt. You will therefore find that there are processes within your systems to purge or roll-up information, thereby losing the detail. I have no doubt that your CIO will have processes in place to archive that information before it is purged, and these archives would probably be stored in a secure location until required (if ever). The issue is not so much the storing of the information, but the retrieval of it. It is highly unlikely that the hardware platform currently implemented is the same as you had ten years ago (this includes computers, backup devices and backup media). It is also unlikely that you will have the same operating system or even application version, and who is going to remember the password from ten years ago, especially as good practice requires that you change passwords every 30 days at a minimum. I would suggest that you ask your CIO (along with the appropriate data owner) to demonstrate that relevant information can be retrieved from 5 or 10 years ago. Note that your Privacy legislation may require you to purge information once the required retention period has passed. Of course, the same applies to your paper storage. If you have paper storage, ask the relevant data owners to provide you with specific records from 5 or 10 years ago. The results might be interesting.

2. You may have to comply with specific legislation based on who you are. If you are a bank, you must comply with banking laws, if a casino, with gambling laws, etc. This is often where Governance legislation falls, to the extent that if you are a public company, you must comply with those

laws. I regret that there is too much diversity to even attempt a discussion of this, however, you need to ensure that your compliance function has this covered, and the appropriate information and guidance is given to your CIO and other relevant management.

3. Standards fall into this third category. This is not about who you are, but whom you choose to be. There are usually no laws forcing you to adopt these standards, but you may choose to adhere to them because of the business you are in and the business you wish to do. For example, you are not forced to follow ISO 9000, but by doing so you have the advantage of improved processes, and perhaps the opening of business doors. Similarly, there is no legislation forcing you to comply with the PCI standard (Payment Card Industry – deals with credit cards and credit card information), but if credit cards and their information form a substantial part of your

business, you will have to comply in order to continue accepting payment in that form. Similarly, you (or your CIO) can choose to comply with CobiT and ITIL or the various IT related ISO standards.

4. Beyond this point compliance tends to be internally focused, and covers the realm of policies, procedures, internal standards and guidelines, and while still part of good Corporate and IT Governance, is perhaps too much detail for this topic of IT Governance for the CEO and members of the board. I would however urge you to remember that failure of your management and staff to comply with internal policies and procedures can possibly result in enormous losses to the business (Barings Bank) and open you up to potential litigation.

So the above dealt with you knowing what you have to comply with. What you also have to do is ensure that you do actually comply. For this you will have to rely on a "positive assurance of compliance", and this you will get from your internal audit function, possibly your external auditors, and perhaps even independent third parties(for example PCI compliance). Your job is to ensure that those assurance givers address compliance, particularly as it relates to your IT functions. This assurance and the reporting thereof should form part of the processes managed by your Risk and Audit committees.

To Do

1.) Ensure that you have a Compliance function that monitors relevant statutory and industry authority bodies, and provides guidance to your CIO and other management about ensuring compliance.
2.) Ensure that you have an assurance function (usually your Internal Audit department) that knows what you have to comply with, and will provide assurance about that compliance.

To Demand

1.) Regular reporting on the status of compliance, through your Audit and Risk Committees. (This of course is not restricted to IT Governance, but can be considered part of Corporate Governance generally.)

2.) Your CIO should demonstrate, or your Internal Audit department should provide assurance that records (paper or electronic) can be retrieved from five to 10 years ago.

Human Behaviour

Now at this point you must be flipping back to the title of the book, and wondering what on earth Human Behaviour has got to do with IT Governance!!! You are not alone in your confusion. While human behaviour is definitely part of the CIO's management responsibility, it probably has very little relevance in its own right to you, as a CEO or member of the Board, particularly concerning IT Governance. Human behaviour is included in this book as an element for the sole reason that it is one of the 6 principles dealt with in ISO/IEC 38500:2008. This principle is summarised in the standard as "IT policies, practices and decisions demonstrate respect for Human Behaviour, including the current and evolving needs of all the 'people in the process'."

The standard then goes on to deal with the Directors processes of Evaluate, Direct and Monitor, all in less than 1 page, which is not very helpful. I have no doubt that there will be many many IT Governance consultants lining up, willing to charge you millions of dollars to help you deal with this very subject, but it is probably not necessary. As stated above, it is your CIO's job to manage his people, and there is plenty of guidance from CobiT, ITIL and other frameworks. Your HR team must also play a role in this function.

What you do have to recognize however, is that it is people that keep your computer systems operating, either your IT guys through the back end and with the supporting infrastructure, or your operations people through the front end, as users of those systems, and there are risks associated with all of these people. Your Risk and Audit committees should deal with these risks, but I will cover some of them here.

1. IT systems very often require very specific skills to maintain and operate. These skills can be scarce, and your CIO needs to identify them, needs to identify dependencies on individuals, and take steps to ensure that there are sufficient people with the appropriate skills to ensure continued operations.

2. Within IT departments there are generally SUPER USERS that have access to everything. A disgruntled super user could cause tremendous damage, either through destruction of data, or through distribution of that data. Your CIO needs to take steps to restrict the fallout if any, and needs to monitor the department and individuals for any signs of trouble.

3. Ergonomics is a term that covers a whole lot of ills. Your CIO probably in conjunction with your Health & Safety team, needs to ensure that use of the computer systems by your staff does not result in things like Carpal Tunnel Syndrome, Eye trouble, and back and neck strain due to badly placed screens and keyboards.

You are probably not going to get involved with the detail (or even the big picture) of the above as it is likely that you have got much better things to do with your precious time. Let your CIO, HR team, and the Risk and Audit Committees get on with managing this sort of stuff, and you get on with doing what you do best, whatever that may be.

Independent Assurance

Even though you may be comfortable with your CIO telling you that he or she is doing a good job, you need to get a second opinion! You will usually get that opinion from your internal and external auditors. All of the documents dealing with IT Governance have Independent Assurance as an element.

If you have an Internal Audit function then they should be in a position to provide you with the assurance about the compliance of IT with its policies, standards and procedures, as well as with generally accepted good practices. Your internal audit function will therefore require specialized IT skills in order to fulfill this function, in order that they are able to provide a competent opinion. Your standard Internal Auditors will not be in a position to engage technically with your IT management.

If your internal audit function does provide you with assurance about your IT department, it is best that they use the same framework in use within IT as a basis for their audit programs. The framework most appropriate for this is the CobiT framework, which includes control objectives and a large number of tests for audit purposes. It also means that both IT and Internal Audit are "singing from the same book" and the process is likely to be a whole lot more productive. Your CIO will know what to expect from Internal Audit, and vice versa.

Similarly, your external auditors are going to want to review your IT systems to the extent that they support your financials. All of the big audit firms have their own IT audit programs, which often bear no resemblance to anything anybody else has.

There are two things that you or your Audit Committee need to ensure. The first is that your external auditors must place reliance on the work of your internal auditors. There are a whole lot of standards and processes in this regard, and you could reduce your external audit fee significantly if they will accept the work done by internal audit.

The second thing to ensure is that if external audit are not placing reliance on internal audit, the work they do must dovetail with the framework in use within IT, in order that it adds value to your ongoing operational IT processes.

There is an additional type of independent assurance that you can place reliance on, and this relates to specialized areas, such as PCI compliance or security audits including activities such as penetration testing. Such assurance from independent third parties can provide you with some comfort that those areas are being dealt with appropriately by your CIO.

Finally, your Internal Audit department should also provide assurance that the IT

Governance processes in place within your organization are appropriate, and that they are being complied with.

To Do

1.) Ensure that you have an Internal Audit function that is able to provide assurance on IT Operational and Governance processes.

To Demand

1.) That your external auditors place reliance on the work that internal audit does.
2.) The work that both internal audit and external audit undertake must add value to the ongoing operations of IT.
3.) Specialized third party assurance should be obtained where appropriate.
4.) Regular reporting of the assurances through your Risk, Audit and IT committees.

Stakeholder Transparency / Reporting

All of the above will be of little value unless it is reported to you. Your IT Governance reports that you place reliance on to ensure that you have fulfilled your obligations in terms of IT Governance should include all of the elements discussed above. It is not envisaged that you get detailed reports at your level, however, having delegated a large portion of your responsibilities to an IT Committee, it would be expected that they would have discussed the issues arising, and provided the Board with a filtered and summarized report, ensuring that it is limited to those items that are of relevance.

The Board in turn, will report to the shareholders and other stakeholders, on a variety of matters, and will include in those reports as much detail as necessary to satisfy those stakeholders that they (the Board) have met their responsibilities concerning IT Governance. No doubt, there will be a section about Corporate Governance in your reports, and the statements about IT Governance should form part of that section.

<u>To Do</u>

1.) In your reports to your stakeholders, in the section where you report on Corporate Governance, include statements relating to IT Governance.

<u>To Demand</u>

1.) That your CIO report to your IT Committee in a format agreed to by that committee, on a regular basis.

2.) Your IT Committee must report to the Board in such a manner that the Board can be satisfied that their obligations regarding IT Governance are met.

Green IT

No, I did not forget about sustainability and your corporate social responsibility. It is just that it has not yet made it onto the IT Governance frameworks, standards and guidelines, but it is only a matter of time before it does. One might question the need for this as part of IT Governance, when it is already covered under the Corporate Governance umbrella. However, similarly to most of the other elements such as Risk and Compliance, specialized IT knowledge may be required to manage this.

The primary areas that can be examined relate to power consumption, resource utilization and disposal and recycling.

While it could also be speculated that if you persuaded the worldwide population of IT Technicians to cut anchovies from their pizzas, that the knock on effect would remove five species from the overfished list, discussion of this does not really fall within the scope of this book.

Power Consumption and the reduction thereof should fall within your overall corporate initiatives. Within IT there are two areas of concern.

The first relates to the actual computing devices themselves. Each PC, Notebook, Server, Storage system, etc. uses electricity. Your CIO should have a program in place to reduce this power consumption, and strategies in this regard could include virtualization of your servers, and management of the power save options and auto shutdown of desktops and peripherals.

The take up of less power hungry hand held devices such as iPads and Tablets could also show a significant reduction in power consumption, provided of course the desktops and laptops are powered down.

The second area of concern relates to cooling, primarily of your server rooms. All the power used by the servers and related equipment generates an enormous amount of heat, and more energy is required to cool down the equipment. Innovative steps to reduce this power usage have been taken, the most notable being Facebook establishing a server farm in Sweden, just south of the Arctic Circle, where the cold outside air does not require power to chill it before it cools the vast numbers of servers.

Resource Usage. One of the primary resources used by IT is of course paper. Reams and reams of paper, whole forests, are used daily to print the reports and documents generated by the ubiquitous computer systems. Do you (or your secretary) receive your email, read it, print it and then file it? It is probably not necessary. The paperless society has been a Utopian dream for quite some time, but has never really materialized. Up until now, that is! It has never been practical to go to a meeting without paper reports, minutes, information packs, etc. Laptops are too cumbersome for everybody to have one open on the boardroom table, and desktops would just be impossible. The iPad and the Tablet are changing all of that. Not only is it possible, but it is also practical and easy to have your documents on hand, on your Tablet at the boardroom table. If you have not done so already, then you should consider doing away with the vast volumes of paper Committee Meeting minutes and Board Packs, and have them loaded onto every Board Member's Tablet. A suitable annotation applet will allow for the addition of notes and comments to the electronic files. Of course, your CIO will have to ensure there is adequate protection over those files, both from a security perspective, and from a retention perspective. Can you imagine if the documents Arthur Anderson (Enron's Auditors – you remember, this is how this all started) shredded were electronic. A simple "delete all" might have had enormous implications.

Similarly, it is likely that you produce, at enormous expense, "Glossy" Annual Financial Statements. If you were to keep them electronic, and make them available to your stakeholders as a download, you could save a fortune.

The cost savings by going paperless are enormous. Paper, toner, equipment costs, power, costs per page, etc would all reduce, and you would be saving trees!!

Going paperless is facilitated where legislation gives electronic documents the same evidentiary weight as paper documents. If your country does not have such legislation, then you should be lobbying for it.

While the target market of this book may still prefer the traditional paperback, it will, initially at least, be published electronically. I hope that this finds you happily using your electronic reader, and whatever you do, please don't print this book, it is at least 100 pages!!

<u>Disposal and Recycling</u> is an area that is easily addressed. Rather than adding to the landfill problem, your CIO should be finding suitable partners that will recycle the metals and plastics, and whole parts where possible, in your old IT equipment. It should of course go without saying that your CIO would have wiped clean any data on the equipment before passing it on for recycling.

<u>To Do</u>

1.) Ensure that IT is included in your corporate Green initiatives and Social responsibility programs.
2.) Ensure that you and your Board set an example, and conduct all the business of the board with electronic documentation.

To Demand

1.) That your CIO report on his Green initiatives.
2.) That your CIO provide you with a strategy to reduce the use of paper within your organization.
3.) That your CIO provide you with the tools and processes that will allow you to conduct board business electronically.

Sarbanes-Oxley and IT Governance

Good old SOX!! You are probably sick to death of this little TLA (Yes, unfortunately another one), especially if you are subject to and bound by it.

So what does SOX have to say about Information Technology and Information Technology Governance? Precisely nothing! Not a word about computer systems, and believe it or not, the word "governance" does not actually appear in the act at all, let alone "IT Governance". Ok, admittedly, it is not exactly "precisely nothing" that is said about "Information Technology". There is a mention in Sec. 601 where an obscene amount of money is appropriated for **"information technology**, security enhancements, and recovery and mitigation activities in light of the terrorist attacks on September 11, 2001". There is no actual mention of what you are required to do with your computer systems.

However, you have paid out millions in consulting fees to consultants and auditors to ensure that your computer systems and your information technology are SOX compliant. How can this be!? It is easy. The consultants and the auditors saw the Act as a potential source of large volumes of recurring income, and they scratched and dug and searched through the Act until they found enough to be able to put the fear of SOX into you and your organization.

The following is what they found.

1.) **SOX 302** requires the CEO and CFO to attest to the accuracy of the financial statements. As it is likely that your financial reports are the result of processing through your computer systems, you need to be certain that the processing is accurate. It also assigns responsibility to you in establishing and maintaining internal controls, designed to ensure material information is reported to you by others, that you have evaluated the effectiveness of the controls within 90 days prior to the report and that you report on your conclusions regarding the effectiveness of those controls.

Quite a lot for you to take on, and this section dovetails with the next. (**SOX 404**). As your results are reported by technology systems, many of those controls will relate to technology and application controls. This is where they make their money, evaluating those controls, usually in the form of an IT General Controls review. Bear in mind, that SOX is primarily interested in these controls in so much as they relate to the presentation of your financial statements. If you refer to the section above on Independent Assurance, this is also what your External Auditors look for. In theory, there should not be any need therefore for any special SOX IT control review. All of it should be covered by your external auditors in any event, and they of course, should place reliance on the work of your internal audit department.

2.) **SOX 404** requires that there is a management responsibility to establish and maintain an internal control structure and procedures for financial reporting, and that there is an assessment at the end of the fiscal period, on the effectiveness of those controls. SOX 404 further requires that the external auditor shall attest to and report on the attestation made by management.

This is different from 302 in that 404 requires management to attest to the effectiveness, whereas 302 requires the CEO and CFO to attest to the accuracy of the financial statements. As stated earlier there is commonality between these two sections, but once again, the focus is on financial reporting.

It should be noted that the SEC issued a guidance document in 2007 that covers internal controls, and specifically mentions IT General Controls, albeit only in support of the financial statements.

When considering your compliance to this section and to 302, you should reflect on the extent to which you are dependent on spreadsheets to produce your financial statements. The more spreadsheets you have, the more at risk you are of having inaccurate reports and the greater the controls will be required to mitigate that risk. In the ideal world, you would wish to have your financial reports printed from your general ledger reporting system, with a single push of a button, without any further processing required. The internal controls would all be within the application and the review thereof becomes relatively simple once an initial assessment is completed. Understandably, you may have many systems as sources of information for your financial reports, which are collated through spreadsheets, but it is preferred to have this merging or consolidation done through controlled automated processes. Business Intelligence and Data Warehouse reporting systems, which gather their data through structured processes will satisfy the need for automated processes. The use of a spreadsheet Macro to automate your reporting is dubious at best, and you can be guaranteed that your auditors will spend many billable hours verifying the accuracy and reliability of those Macros and spreadsheets.

3.) **SOX 409** covers "Real Time Issuer Disclosures" and this requires that you report on a "rapid and current basis" any material changes to your financial status or operations. The impact of this on your IT systems is that you need to ensure that they produce information that is reliable, accurate and timeous, particularly in terms of financial reporting. It is no good if it takes you four months to produce your quarterly reports. Your operational systems in any event should allow you to establish the status of your operations so that you or your management can respond accordingly. If it takes too long for you to get the information, operational or financial, regardless of any Governance requirement, you will find yourself battling to manage your business.

4.) **SOX 802** deals with the alteration, falsification and destruction of records, and applies criminal penalties to this. In addition corporate audit records are required to be kept for five years. As far as IT is concerned, this has an impact on record retention and data recovery as discussed in the compliance section above. This section generously adds to your obligations about the retention of your audit records.

This section will have an impact on the work of your Internal Audit department, particularly in terms of work done towards attestation of your system of internal controls, as well as work done that the external auditors have placed reliance on. Your Internal and External Auditors will have to keep all working papers, audit trails, evidence, etc., much of which will be electronic, for five years.

After looking at those four sections of the Sarbanes-Oxley Act, you should have realized that most of what they require in terms of your Information Technology is what you should be, and probably have been doing for many years. Your Internal and External Auditors would have been evaluating the above as part of their standard operations. (At least, they should have been.)The Act just formalizes and regulates these processes, and assigns criminal liability if you do not comply. Compliance with Sarbanes-Oxley in terms of IT Governance, should not be too difficult, because most of it is just good practice anyway. If, as part of your IT Governance processes, you have chosen to follow the CobiT framework, (remember that CobiT means **Control** Objectives for Information Technology), you will have covered most of the IT requirements for your system of Internal Controls, and as far as the

Act is concerned, you will have covered far more than the absolute minimum requirement.

Thus after a mere ten pages of dealing with the dreaded SOX, in addition to the copious volumes you have already gone through, one would hope that you have gleaned enough knowledge to satisfy yourself that your IT systems comply.

Conclusion

This book has tried to be as brief as possible, while at the same time, providing you with sufficient knowledge to enable you to satisfy yourself that you understand what is required of you in terms of IT Governance. You should also be able to guide your various organizational structures towards demonstrating and documenting that due diligence and good practices have been followed in the management of your IT Operations.

You will probably find that your CIO is mostly doing what is right, and all that will be required is the formalization of structures, processes and documentation relating to IT Governance. IT people are notoriously bad at documentation, and this will probably be the most difficult part to implement, and maintain.

You will also have noted that many of the processes around IT Governance should already be in place as part of your Corporate Governance processes. In particular, the elements of Value Delivery, Risk Management, Compliance and Independent Assurance should be applicable to all your operations, and not just especially for Information Technology.

Remember that IT has been singled out for special Governance treatment because it is deeply intertwined into the very heart of your business operations and the financial reporting. It is often a significant portion of an organization's operating and capital costs.

It has also had a reputation in the past as being a deep dark hole where endless resources have been thrown, with no tangible benefit. Projects have had enormous cost overruns and on completion, have not delivered the promised benefits, or have been abandoned before completion. It has been a specialized field of knowledge where slick operators (internal and external) have been able to pull the wool over everybody's eyes and get away with murder.

No more!

PostScript

Given that technology changes at a rapid rate, it is a field that requires constant updates. In that spirit, in an effort to keep you up to date, and of course, to provide the author with a recurring source of income, a website has been established that will publish IT and Governance related articles geared towards CEOs and Members of the Board. At the bottom of the section, you will find the address for this website.

You will of course have to register to download any articles. Being aware of the privacy issues around personal information, this registration will not require such details, but will request some geographic and role information. You will also be offered the opportunity to subscribe to monthly articles for a nominal annual fee. A third party will handle payments (thereby absolving the author of any PCI or other responsibility) but your email address will be required to facilitate notifications and correspondence.

Website http://www.ITforTheBoard.com